MEMOIR OF COL. THOMAS KNOWLTON, OF ASHFORD, CONNECTICUT

ASHBEL WOODWARD

Published by Left of Brain Books

Copyright © 2021 Left of Brain Books

ISBN 978-1-396-32006-4

First Edition

All rights reserved. No part of this publication may be reproduced, distributed, or transmitted in any form or by any means, including photocopying, recording, or other electronic or mechanical methods, without the prior written permission of the publisher, except in the case of brief quotations embodied in critical reviews and certain other noncommercial uses permitted by copyright law. Left of Brain Books is a division of Left of Brain Onboarding Pty Ltd.

THE BATTLE AT BUNKER'S HILL.

MEMOIR.

THE reputation men leave behind them depends materially upon circumstances unconnected with their services or worth. Where individuals have acted an important part in moulding the history of their time, posterity, by oft-repeated siftings and reviews, will in the end generally mete out to each the proper measure of credit.

Still, not a few brave men who sacrificed fortune and life to secure our national independence,—men held in high estimation by the most honored of their contemporaries,—have been allowed a very inadequate place in the national records and the national remembrance. Some are forgotten because their acts of heroism were performed in the shadows cast by greater names. Others achieved too much to pass into oblivion, yet fall far short of receiving their deserts through the modesty or indifference of those to whom their reputation was more immediately intrusted. This, we think, is true of Col. Knowlton. We believe that the position has not been awarded to him in the history of the colonial and revolutionary periods, to which his sagacity and valor, his patriotism and distinguished public services entitle him.

Col. Thomas Knowlton was born in the town of West Boxford, Mass., November, 1740. The church records of that place show that he was baptized on the thirtieth day of November, and as the ceremony of baptism was then almost invariably performed on the eighth day after birth, we may infer that he was born on the twenty-second of that month. The Knowlton family were of English origin, and among the earliest settlers of Massachusetts. During the boyhood of Thomas, his father William Knowlton removed from Boxford to the town of Ashford, in the province of Connecticut, where he purchased a farm of four hundred acres.

Not long after the commencement of the "Last French War," in 1755, Knowlton began his military career by enlisting as a private in the company commanded by Capt. Durkee. He continued in the army about four years, and was successively promoted to the rank of sergeant, ensign, and lieutenant, holding the last office in the campaign of 1760, which was signalized by the capture of Canada from the French.

He was present at the battle of Wood Creek, fought in the month of August, 1758. It was here that Major Putnam, having been captured by an Indian warrior, was tied to a tree, where, during a considerable part of the fight, he was exposed to the fire of both friends and foes. The circumstances of the contest relating more particularly to young Knowlton, as narrated by his son, are these: A scouting party, embracing with others the company of Capt. Durkee, had been sent out from the English army to intercept the French and Indian stragglers who were thought to be ranging the forests in the vicinity. While thus engaged they found at Wood Creek an encampment bearing marks of recent occupation. The discovery of kettles and various other articles secreted among the neighboring bogs and brush, induced the belief that the enemy designed to return. Accordingly the Provincials took possession of the grounds and prepared to receive them. But after the lapse of a day or two, a party of English, while ascending the creek on a fishing excursion, encountered a couple of French boats descending. On espying the character of the new comers, the French turning about rowed rapidly up the stream. Feeling that it would be idle to delay any longer in the hope of surprising the enemy, now that their location was known, the Provincials abandoned this position of security to seek the foe. The attempt was full of peril, for the route lay through a heavy forest rendered almost impassable by the dense growth of brakes and underwood. While cautiously advancing in single file, a storm of bullets was suddenly showered upon them by an ambuscade of French and Indians. So thick was the undergrowth that not a foe was visible, the musketry and the smoke wreaths alone revealing their deadly lurking places. The English sought shelter behind the trunks of trees, fighting in a great measure independently of each other.

At an early stage of the conflict the attention of young Knowlton was attracted by a quivering among the brakes, and a moment after he saw an Indian crawling stealthily on hands and knees into the path just formed by the footsteps of the English. He immediately shot the Indian, and having reloaded his musket, sprang forward to secure his scalp for a trophy. Just as he reached the victim ten or twelve Indians jumped up from the grass on all sides of him, each beckoning to the lad to come to his arms as a prisoner. Not at all intimidated by this closing circle of savage foes, the boy-soldier, with a boldness and dexterity that for a moment paralyzed their energies, shot down the nearest warrior, and, bounding over his prostrate body, regained his comrades in safety, though pursued by a shower of balls. Meanwhile the action had become general. Both parties fought desperately, and success alternated from side to side. At length the troops had become so scattered and commingled among the brakes that all regularity was lost, each one managing and fighting for himself. At this stage of the conflict, Knowlton, on entering a small open space, saw a Frenchman enter on the opposite side. Each snapped his musket, and both muskets missed fire. As neither of them had bayonets, the Frenchman endeavored to draw a dirk, but before he could succeed, Knowlton had clasped him around the waist and now exerted all his strength to throw him. But the endurance of the large and powerful man proved an overmatch for the immature though active boy. Knowlton was thrown, but at this juncture an American soldier fortunately entered the opening when their antagonist begged for quarters. Having re-primed his gun Knowlton and his companion began to lead away the prisoner, when he sprang from their hands and attempted to escape, but ere he had run many steps his flight was stopped forever by a ball from the musket of Knowlton.

The two associates in this adventure, from whom the rest had become separated by retreat, now attempted to rejoin the main body of troops. After running in different directions, and being shot at several times, they gained the rear of the English. During the engagement Knowlton's coat was perforated on the shoulder by a ball, but he escaped unharmed. For the valor here exhibited he was promoted to a sergeancy, and before the close of the war was raised to the rank of lieutenant.

When we reflect that such heroism and judgment were displayed by a youth of less than eighteen years, we are not surprised to find him, at the maturer age of thirty-six, accounted the first officer of his grade in the American army.

He was present at the capture of Ticonderoga and performed other services in the campaigns of 1759-60 which brought the French and Indian war to a close.

Upon the commencement of hostilities between Spain and England in 1762, Knowlton sailed with the Provincials under Gen. Lyman to join Lord

Albemarle for the reduction of Havana. After a long and brave defence the Spanish surrendered. But the climate proved more disastrous to the Americans and English than the batteries of the enemy. When the place capitulated, August 13th, disease had already made frightful ravages among our men. Comparatively a small part surviving the hazards of the expedition were spared to return to their homes. On the return passage Knowlton was challenged to fight a duel by a British officer, whom he had rebuked for some offence perpetrated while in liquor. But on maturer reflection, either becoming convinced of his error or fearful of encountering so cool and determined an adversary, the Englishman withdrew the challenge and apologized for his haste.

Col. Knowlton had married, April 5, 1759, Miss Anna, daughter of Sampson Keyes, of Ashford. Subsequently to the general pacification which succeeded the fall of Havana, he followed the quiet pursuits of agriculture at home in Ashford. There he continued to reside in the bosom of an affectionate family till the growing alienation between the Colonies and the Mother Country blazed into deadly hostility at Lexington and Concord. During this interval of repose he sustained among his fellow-townsmen a high character for honesty and discretion. The demoralizing influences of camp life had passed over his head as harmlessly as the bullets of the Indian foe. Although not a professor of piety he was a punctual attendant at church, and was ever ready to lend a helping hand to encourage enterprises of benevolence and humanity. A generous nature and expansive sympathies raising him above the narrow bigotry of sects, prompted him to take a bold though modest stand against the religious intolerance at that time in many parts of New England unfortunately too rife. A well authenticated incident, which happened a few years before the Revolution, illustrates our point. As he was riding on one occasion past the Presbyterian church, he observed a crowd gathered around the whipping-post, planted, according to the harsh usages of the day, in the vicinity. On inquiry he ascertained that a culprit was to be flogged for non-attendance at church and the non-payment of tithes. When the sentence was read preparatory to the infliction of the punishment, he noticed the omission of the usual clause requiring the stripes to be applied to the bare back. Taking advantage of the inadvertence of the scribe, he threw his own overcoat over the shoulders of the victim whereby the torture was greatly mitigated.

At the age of thirty-three he was appointed one of the selectmen of the town. This was spoken of at the time as quite a wonder, for silvery hair and ripe experience were then thought indispensable to the proper discharge of the duties of that august office. Young America has seriously encroached upon the notions entertained by our forefathers.

When the tidings of the conflict at Lexington reached Ashford, Knowlton held no military command. But a spirit like his required no urging to a scene of action where the cause of liberty had been baptized in the blood of his countrymen. Leaving his farm-business just as it was, and bidding adieu to his family, he hurried with gun and well filled powder horn to the rendezvous of the Ashford company. Had he been desirous of an excuse for remaining at home, the circumstances of his situation would have afforded several. His wife, whose love for her husband exceeded her devotion to the cause of independence, exhausted all the art and ingenuity of womanly persuasion to detain him from the war. A numerous family of young and dependent children appealed in mute eloquence to the affections of a father's heart. The military affairs of the township were entirely in the hands of others, while an important civil office seemingly demanded his attention at home. None of these considerations, however, weighed a straw when balanced in the scale against the momentous interests now to be decided by the arbitrament of the sword.

The company formed at Ashford, being destitute of a captain, proceeded to fill the vacancy by ballot. Knowlton had joined as a private and offered no claim for the situation. Yet so great was the reputation for bravery, prudence, and sagacity, that had followed him home from the French war, that he was unanimously selected for the post. This company was the first which entered Massachusetts from a sister colony. How honorable and useful a part it acted there will appear presently.

Knowlton was the favorite officer of Putnam, and such confidence did the veteran general repose in the accuracy of his judgment, that he invariably consulted him in matters of importance. A short time before the Provincials took possession of Bunker's Hill, Putnam came to his quarters and in a private interview developed the plan of seizing and fortifying that height. Knowlton wholly disapproved of the project, insisting that it would probably prove fatal to the American troops engaged in it; for the British, by landing at Charlestown Neck under the protection of the floating batteries and ships of war, could cut off from the hill all supplies of provisions and ammunition, besides rendering retreat extremely hazardous if not impossible. "Still," he continued, "if you are determined to go upon the hill I shall accompany you with my men and exert myself to the uttermost." This conversation was overheard by Edward Keyes, of Ashford, a private in the company, who stood sentry at the door and listened with the intense curiosity of a raw young soldier of seventeen. He narrated the incident to the informant of the writer. As affairs turned, the recklessness of Lord Howe and his contempt for the American army, saved them in a measure from the catastrophe which Capt. Knowlton and other prudent officers had anticipated.

After many debates the scheme of Gen. Putnam prevailed, and it was determined to hazard the fortunes of an engagement on the Charlestown peninsula. On the night of June 16th, a body of about one thousand men under the command of Col. Prescott, following the glimmer of dark lanterns, crossed the neck. Here they overtook several wagon loads of intrenching tools, the sight of which first apprized the inferior officers and privates of the design of their darksome march. A controversy now arose as to the proper hill to be fortified. Bunker Hill, the only one on the peninsula then designated by a distinctive name, was explicitly mentioned in the order. But the remoteness of that elevation from Boston, induced them, in the face of the instructions from the committee of safety, to move farther on to the eminence afterwards known as Breed's Hill, though not so high as the former by fifty feet. Owing to this dispute it was nearly midnight before the sward was broken. Capt. Knowlton commanded a fatigue party of about two hundred Connecticut men.[1] These were the first to strike the spade, and toiled unceasingly till the grey light of morning revealed to the astonished Britons the ominous defences reared, while the familiar cry, "All's well," had lulled them to sleep. So vigorously had the work been pushed that by break of day a strong redoubt had been thrown up, flanked on the left by a breastwork extending down the hill in a northerly direction, and terminating a few rods south of an impassable slough. The rear of the breastwork was connected with the redoubt by a narrow sally-port. Beyond the slough, the tongue of land about two hundred

---

[1] The Bunker's Hill Roll of the Ashford company contains ninety-six names inclusive of officers.

and fifty yards in width, lying on the southern side of the Mystic River, was undefended. The configuration of the peninsula rendered the occupation of this unguarded point by the American troops indispensable to their success and even their safety. The enemy by marching along the bank of the stream could gain the rear of the redoubt and slay or capture its defenders at a blow.

Accordingly, while the British, after landing at Moreton's Point, were partaking of refreshments and waiting for reinforcements, Capt. Knowlton, with the Connecticut troops under his command, was ordered to take possession of this pass. Here he adopted a novel mode of fortification, the efficacy of which far exceeded the anticipations of its projector. A post and rail fence already stretched across the field from the river to the road. The soldiers, taking rails from other fences in the neighborhood, built a second fence parallel to the first, and filled the intervening space with freshly mown hay.

It may seem strange to some that the command at a point of such vital importance should be intrusted to Capt. Knowlton, when there were other officers on the hill of superior rank, who might feel aggrieved at such an assignment of this post of honor as well as danger. The reason is to be found in the thorough confidence which Gen. Putnam reposed in him. Years before they had often marched and fought side by side. On long expeditions through the wilderness, and on the battle-field, Putnam had learned to appreciate the qualities of the youthful hero. After the lapse of a decade they again stood together upon the verge of a bloody conflict. The strip of hard upland bordering on the Mystic, the key to the American works on the peninsula, must be guarded at all hazards. Gen. Putnam, ignoring considerations of titular pre-eminence, insisted that Capt. Knowlton was just the man for the place, and it was accordingly given to him.

Col. Stark, coming upon the ground at a later hour, also took post behind the rail fence, at the extremity towards the redoubt; the three commanders, Prescott, Stark, and Knowlton, in their several positions, fighting the battle independently of each other.

The British were drawn up in two wings, the left under Gen. Pigot moving with steady step against the redoubt, and the right led by Lord Howe in person, against the rail fence. Lord Howe looked with contempt both upon the breastwork of hay and rails, and the backwoodsmen behind it. He fully expected that its defenders would fly in dismay at the first shot, leaving him free to attack the main body in flank, while Gen. Pigot carried the works in front. But he sadly mistook the reception that awaited him. Reserving their fire till the enemy came within six or eight rods, the Provincials poured upon them incessant volleys. Capt. Knowlton, divested of coat, walked along the line in front of his men, encouraging them both by example and by words. He repeatedly loaded and discharged with deadly aim his own faithful musket, till it was struck by a cannon ball and knocked into the form of a semicircle. In this shape it was carried from the ground, and afterwards remained many years in possession of the family, but now is unfortunately lost. Notwithstanding the great superiority of the British right wing, in numbers, discipline, and accoutrements, they proved a most unequal match for the Americans opposed to them. The latter resting their guns upon the rails took deliberate aim. The enemy fell by scores at every volley till hundreds lay in heaps upon the earth. Yet as huge gaps were opened others stepped bravely in to fill the vacant places and share the same fate. Very many of the companies lost from three-fourths to nine-tenths of their men, and of several scarcely half a dozen escaped. While the assailants were thus slaughtered, the defenders of the rampart remained unharmed, partly because the artillery of Lord Howe proved useless, being stopped by a marsh, and partly because the closely packed grass was impervious to musket balls. Besides, as the British took no aim, their shot mostly passed over the heads of the Americans, as shown by the fact that the upper limbs and foliage of several trees standing a little in the rear were completely riddled, while the trunks and lower limbs were hardly grazed. At length Lord Howe, with the remnant of the column that shortly before had moved proudly on the field, as if to certain victory, was compelled to retreat.

The enemy had been repulsed at every point; yet, nothing daunted, Lord Howe marshaled the troops for a fresh attack. A second time his division marched calmly and boldly as before, over the bodies of fallen comrades, against the rail fence. Restraining with difficulty the impetuosity inspired by success, the Americans impatiently withheld their fire till the space between the hostile armies was narrowed to six rods. Suddenly the crash of musketry resounded along the lines, and the messengers of death leaped from hundreds of muzzles at once. The slaughter of officers was frightful. Lord Howe, seemingly possessed of a charmed life, was three times left alone, so great was the destruction around him. Human fortitude could not long face a murderous fire like this. Despite the exertions of Howe, who sought the thickest danger, endeavoring by gestures and words to rekindle hope in the hearts of the despairing, the shattered columns reeled, broke, and fled.

Gen. Clinton, having watched from Copp's Hill the progress of the battle, had discovered the vulnerable point of the American lines. Stung to madness by the carnage of the very flower of the army, he crossed over to the peninsula, and as a volunteer joined the dejected troops. Two disastrous repulses had convinced the British generals that the rail fence was impregnable. The third time, therefore, a different plan of attack was adopted. Instead of storming the redoubt in front, they determined to take it in flank through the open space between the breastwork and fence. While Howe with a part of his wing made a feint of repeating his attack upon the fortified fence, another part brought several cannon to enfilade the breastwork on the left of the redoubt. As the troops behind it were protected only in front, they were compelled to seek refuge in the enclosure. As the British advanced with fixed bayonets the Americans greeted them with a final volley, for their ammunition was now exhausted. While the soldiers of Howe were pouring into the redoubt on the northern side, Clinton and Pigot had come up and were assailing it on the south and east. For a short time the Americans contended against the bayonets of the foe with the stocks of their muskets and whatever missiles they could seize. Prescott was soon forced to order a retreat.

While the main body were making their escape, Knowlton and his compeers resolutely maintained their position behind the fence, thus frustrating Lord Howe's design of cutting off the retreat of the Americans. As the division of Prescott passed the fortified fence which was one hundred and ninety yards in the rear of the breastwork that formed a continuation of the redoubt, Col. Stark's regiment, whose ammunition was also expended, joined in with it. Knowlton now ordered the four companies under his command to withdraw from the post which they had defended so successfully. Fortunately they had double the number of cartridges of the other troops, having brought them from Connecticut. Retiring slowly, and making the most effective use of their extra ammunition, they formed the rear-guard of the Americans in their retreat. Without doubt the obstinate bravery of Knowlton's division, rendered effective, as it was, by a plentiful supply of powder and shot, saved many who but for their interposition never could have escaped from the peninsula.

As the Ashford company, after leaving the rail-fence, was passing near a field-piece which had been loaded by the Americans, and then abandoned in that condition, Robert Hale, one of its members, rushed from the ranks, and seizing a brand discharged it. The diversified fragments of metal which had been substituted for a ball, mowed a wide swath through the British ranks. In the momentary confusion which ensued, Hale slipped away from his perilous position and regained his comrades in safety.

Thus it will be seen that Knowlton's company was the first to enter Massachusetts from a sister colony; that the four companies placed for the time under his command were the only troops from abroad to go upon Breed's Hill on the night of the 17th; that after toiling for hours in throwing up the redoubt, they removed to a new position where they shared the privilege of twice repulsing Lord Howe; and finally that they were the last to leave the scene of conflict. Notwithstanding all this exposure but three are marked as killed on the roll of the Ashford company.[2]

For his gallantry in this engagement, Knowlton was promoted by Congress to the rank of Major, and was thenceforward generally esteemed the first officer of his grade in the army. A gentleman of Boston, likewise, out of admiration for his conduct, presented to him a *gold laced hat*, an *elegant sash*, and *gold breast-plate*. The breast-plate is still in possession of the family.

Col. Burr, a keen judge of men and brilliant officer, as all must acknowledge, notwithstanding the odium cast upon him by the later transactions of his life, became acquainted with Knowlton and was singularly

---

[2] In the account here given of the part taken by Col. Knowlton in the battle of Banker's Hill, we have placed great reliance upon the facts collected by the late Wm. W. Marcy, Esq. Mr. Marcy possessed qualities of mind which eminently fitted him for historical investigations. Having married a grand-daughter of Col. Knowlton, he took a deep interest in the events of his life, and was untiring in the inquiries he made among the survivors of the Ashford Company who fought on the Hill, to ascertain minutely the part the Colonel there acted.

We would also here acknowledge our indebtedness to the manuscripts intrusted to the writer, by Capt. Miner Knowlton of the U. S. Army, who has been assiduous in collecting every known fact in regard to the life and services of his distinguished relative.

captivated both by his military talent, and the qualities of his open and fearless nature. Not long before his death, in speaking of the friend of his youth, Burr said, "I had a full account of the battle from Knowlton's own lips, and believe if the chief command had been entrusted to him, the issue would have proved more fortunate." When the objection was raised that he ought not to be placed before Prescott and Stark, Burr observed, that "such was not his intention,—that an able and efficient *general* commander was wanted, as *they*, like Knowlton, had particular posts to defend; and great fault rests somewhere for not bringing to them proper support." Alluding to the rapidity of his promotion, he remarked, "It was impossible to promote such a man too rapidly."

During the subsequent winter, while the Americans were beleaguering Boston, Major Knowlton was stationed with Gen. Putnam at Cambridge. With by far the greater number, the time passed wearily, because the monotony of camp-life was seldom relieved by stirring incidents. The soldiers were discontented, the officers gloomy, and even Congress exhibited many signs of anxious foreboding. At this time the daring and successful exploit of a few Americans contributed to revive the drooping hopes of the army. A deserter from the enemy communicated the information that several English officers were quartered in the scattering houses at Charlestown that had escaped the conflagration of June 17th. Gen. Washington, having conferred with Putnam, directed Maj. Knowlton to cross over to the peninsula, with the deserter, and from personal inspection ascertain the truthfulness of the statement. The command was executed the next night. On the second evening (February 8th,) between the hours of eight and nine, Knowlton proceeded from Cobble Hill with one hundred men from the first brigade, and a like number from Frye's brigade, being determined, if possible, to burn the houses and capture the officers. No one can appreciate the delicacy or danger of the undertaking unless acquainted with the situation of the peninsula at the time. Bunker's Hill was garrisoned by the main force under Gen. Howe, while Charlestown Neck was strongly guarded. The only way of access was by the narrow mill-dam extending from east to west across the bay, and so low that the top was frequently buried beneath the tides. Yet over this slender pathway the Americans marched in single file, with Knowlton at the head, toward the gaping jaws of the British lion. On reaching the guard-house, the sentinel advanced with presented bayonet. Knowlton, still leading the way, thrust it aside with the left hand and run him through the body with the right so suddenly that not the least alarm was given. The inmates were surprised and captured. When the men had been so arranged as to secure a safe retreat, they began to fire the buildings. As the flames darted upward, the enemy on the hill, imagining that a formidable army was about to attack them, opened a heavy cannonade from the fort. Knowlton's party persevered till seventeen scattered houses were in a blaze, he himself remaining behind the rest to start afresh one of the fires which they in their hurry had left. The whole number then returned by the way they came, without the injury of a man, although thundered upon by the artillery on the hill.

Lieut. Trafton, a member of the party, afterwards observed in conversation, "It was considered at the time an operation of great hazard, especially in securing a retreat; but we had entire confidence in the officer commanding, and that he could effect it if any officer in the army could."

The garrison on Bunker Hill were not the only frightened ones. A theatre had been fitted up in the city, early in the season, which was much frequented by officers and tories. On the evening in question, a farce, written by Gen. Burgoyne, and entitled "The Blockade of Boston," was to be performed as an after-piece. The curtain had just arisen, and the character representing Washington, equipped with a mammoth wig and sword, and followed by a ragged orderly sergeant armed with a rusty musket seven or eight feet long, were about to commence the entertainment of the crowded assembly at the expense of the besiegers, when a *genuine* serjeant hurried upon the stage, announcing that "the Yankees were attacking Bunker's Hill." This was thought to be a part of the acting, till Gen. Howe gave the order, "Officers, to your alarm posts!" Great confusion followed. A rush was made for the door, the ladies shrieking, and the men, whose enthusiasm in many instances had been wrought up to a high point by frequent potations from the punch bowl, muttering their aspirations for the Yankees, in language too sulphureous to bear repetition by the sober.

An order, now extant, signed by Gen. Washington and dated at Head-Quarters, Cambridge, Feb. 28, 1776, directing the Paymaster-General to pay to Maj. Knowlton so many pounds, lawful money, to purchase arms for the use of the twentieth regiment *under his command,* shows that although holding only the commission of Major, he was in actual command of a regiment.

After the British evacuated Boston, Knowlton proceeded to join the army then engaged in the defence of New York. On the way he made a short visit to his family in Ashford, and while there paid off his troops in scrip. A regiment called the rangers was now raised by the selection of the choicest men from the Connecticut troops. Knowlton was commissioned Lt. Colonel, and the command of this regiment, which had been appointed expressly for desperate and delicate services, was given to him.

Before the battle of Long Island, Gen. Putnam entered zealously into a scheme for the destruction of the British fleet in the harbor by means of fire-ships. The time for the execution of the project had been fixed; simultaneously Knowlton and Mercer were to make a descent upon Staten Island. A succession of unpropitious events thwarted the design of burning the ships; but the failure of that part of the enterprise did not deter Knowlton and Mercer from attempting to accomplish theirs. Twice they made preparations for crossing the straits, but were prevented, once by tempestuous weather, and once by deficiency of boats.

At the battle of Long Island the rangers were sent to reinforce Lord Stirling. All at once the firing in that quarter ceased. Convinced in his own mind that Stirling had surrendered, Knowlton instantly ordered a retreat into the lines, which was effected with great celerity, and just in time to save them from a large body of British Light Horse, who a moment after galloped to the field. Thus the accurate judgment and quick decision of the Colonel rescued the regiment from a sword wielded that day with pitiless ferocity.

Subsequently to this disastrous battle, while the Americans were occupying the peninsula of New York, and the British the city of Brooklyn, Gen. Washington was extremely anxious to learn the strength and contemplated movements of the enemy. He accordingly summoned a council of officers in order that they might deliberate together on a matter of so great importance. They thought it necessary to send a man into the heart of the British camp, provided any one of proper qualifications could be found, who was willing to go. Col. Knowlton was charged with the superintendence of the enterprise. When he proposed the plan to his officers, Nathan Hale, of South Coventry, Conn., one of the captains in Knowlton's regiment, was the only one ready to volunteer his services. The brilliant and versatile talents of Hale led his colonel to recommend him to Washington, as a person eminently fitted for the perilous task. The offer was accepted by the commander-in-chief. The skill, the fortitude, and the heroic self-devotion exhibited by the youthful martyr, are familiar to all.

We now approach the closing scene in the career of the brave Knowlton. The calamities on Long Island, the shameful flight at Kip's Bay, the series of misfortunes about New York, that for several months had uninterruptedly pursued the American flag, and, moreover, the wretched condition of the troops, produced an all-pervading gloom throughout the camp and the country. A large and thoroughly disciplined army, commanded by experienced officers, amply furnished with the munitions of war, and flushed with successive victories, threatened to exterminate the cause of independence. Had not the love of liberty been a deathless flame in the hearts of our forefathers, they must in this hour of culminating disasters have abandoned hostilities in despair. But an unconquerable spirit animated them. From the furnace of affliction they came forth, scorched and bleeding it is true, yet purified, and ready to dare more and suffer more for what they had already dared and suffered so much.

The main body of our army was now occupying the fortified camp extending along the upper part of New York Island. Col. Knowlton, ever on the alert, had been sent with a detachment of one hundred and fifty men, to watch the movements of the enemy. Keeping the corps concealed, he directed two of the soldiers to reconnoitre the lines. They were ordered to proceed stealthily and without noise so as to avoid giving the slightest alarm. On approaching undiscovered within fair gun-shot of the enemy, yielding to a mad desire they fired upon them, and then hurried back to the main body. For disobedience to orders they were severely reprimanded by the colonel. Close at the heels of the scouts followed six hundred British. Knowlton arranged the detachment behind a field-fence, but finding that the enemy, four times superior in number, were bent on gaining the rear and cutting off retreat, he withdrew to a piece of woods, where he fought with great resolution till overpowered and driven back by numerical superiority. In the mean time a reinforcement was sent from the American camp, under Major Leitch, with orders to join Knowlton and gain the rear of the British, while a feigned attack was made upon them in front. As the troops advanced for the false attack, the enemy ran down the hill to gain a more advantageous position. While these manœuvres were executed in front, the main body having made a circuit to strike the rear, being ignorant of the change in the disposition of the forces, came upon the enemy's flank. A brisk contest ensued, in which both sides were reinforced and fought with great determination, till the enemy were driven from the woods into the plain and pursued for some distance. In the hottest of the engagement Maj. Leitch was borne from the field mortally wounded. Shortly after, Col. Knowlton, while bravely leading the attack, was shot through the head, and survived only an hour. His eldest son, a lad who had not yet seen his sixteenth birth-day, was in the same battle and fired several rounds before he heard the sad intelligence. When word was brought that his father was dying, he hurried to his side. The hero, gasping in the death struggle, clasped his hand for a final adieu, and thus addressed him. "You see, my son, I am mortally wounded; you can do me no good; go, fight for your country." Do the pages of history furnish an instance of sublimer patriotism? As the agonies of dissolution were racking the body of a soldier thus snatched from life in the midst of the glow, and pomp, and hope of early manhood, solicitude for the country for whose deliverance he had fought so often and so valiantly, excluded all narrower or more personal thoughts. Col. Reed, an eye witness of the scene, says, "All his inquiry was whether we had driven in the enemy."

In the general orders of the next day, Gen. Washington says, "The gallant and brave Col. Knowlton, who would have been *an honor to any country*, having fallen yesterday while gloriously fighting, Capt. Brown is to take command of the party lately led by Col. Knowlton."

When the news of the loss of her favorite son reached Ashford, deep and heart-felt sorrow pervaded the town. Every house became an habitation of mourning not less than if one of its own inmates, having gone to the wars, was to return no more forever. Even the man who was supposed to be his only enemy, wept like a child.

The writer of this sketch, whose boyhood was passed in Ashford, well remembers the enthusiasm and affection with which the surviving co-temporaries of Col. Knowlton always spoke of him.

In person he was six feet high, erect and elegant in figure, and formed more for activity than strength. He had light complexion, dark hair, and eyes of deep spiritual beauty. His literary education was confined to the narrow routine of studies then taught in the common schools. Yet the possession of an intellect naturally bright, and quick to profit by the experiences and associations of military life, caused his companionship to be sought by the most cultivated. He was courteous and affable in manners, and wholly free from ostentation and egotism. Ever willing to bestow on others the praise due to their merit, he received the applause due to himself without a murmur of dissent. Calm and collected in battle, and, if necessity required, ready to lead where any could be found to follow—he knew no fear of danger. The favorite of superior officers, the idol of his soldiers and fellow-townsmen, he fell universally lamented. Half a century afterwards, a grandson of Col. Knowlton, travelling in New Hampshire, casually met a Revolutionary soldier, who, in rehearsing the story of his campaigns, mentioned the engagement at Harlem Heights where he fought under Knowlton. On learning that the young man was a descendant of his former commander, the old gentleman pressed him with invitations to pass the night at his house, nor would he listen to any excuse. The confidence that he had reposed in Knowlton, when they were companions in arms, was seemingly unlimited. He remarked, that "the colonel was the mildest and most agreeable man he ever knew—that nothing of a rough or harsh nature ever passed his lips—that he was universally respected by those under his command as well as those associated with him." Such were the sentiments with regard to Col. Knowlton invariably entertained by those who knew him.

And what has been done by our country to honor the name of the man who, at the first note of warning, drew the sword for liberty, never laying it aside till his arm was cold in death? Have a grateful people, living in the midst of the prosperity purchased at so great cost of revolutionary suffering and revolutionary blood, reared for him any monument to tell the world that her defenders are embalmed in perpetual remembrance? Has the government of the United States whose faithful soldier he was, or the city of New York whose soil he died to defend, or the Commonwealth of Connecticut that points with pride to his name as one of her brightest jewels, ever offered this slight tribute of filial duty? To all such inquiries we must answer in the negative. The only monument to his memory is a very plain cenotaph, planted by the hand of affection in the cemetery at Ashford, and cut with this inscription: "This monument is erected in memory of Col. Thomas Knowlton and his wife. That brave colonel, in defence of his country, fell in battle, Sep. 16th 1776, at Harlem Heights, Island of N. York, Æ 36 years."

Col. Knowlton was buried with military honors near the road leading from Kingsbridge to the city.

KEY TO THE BATTLE AT BUNKER'S HILL.

1	Lieut-col. Parker	2	Sam.l McClintock D.D.	3	Maj. Moore	4
5	Maj. Knowlton	6	Col. Wm. Prescott	7	Gen. Joseph Warren	8
9	Gen. Sir Wm. Howe	10	Maj. Small	11	Col. Abercrombie	12
13	Lieut. Pitcairn	14	Lieut. Lord Rawdon	15	Col. Tho.s Gardener	16
17	Lieut. Grosvenor					

Gen. Israel Putnam
Maj. Knowlton
Gen. Sir Wm. Howe
Maj. Pitcairn
Lieut. Grosvenor

KEY TO THE BATTLE AT BUNKER'S HILL.

No. 1. *General Israel Putnam* was born in Salem, Massachusetts, 7th January, 1718; he was married at an early age, and removed to Pomfret, Connecticut. In 1755 he was appointed captain of a provincial regiment, and served for some time on the frontiers and in Canada, and rose to the rank of lieutenant-colonel. On the breaking out of the revolutionary war he repaired immediately to Boston, and was appointed a major-general. He was engaged in the battle of Bunker's Hill, and held an important command till December, 1779, when he had a paralytic attack, from the effects of which he suffered till the 29th of May, 1790, when he died at Brooklyn, Connecticut.

No. 2. *Lieutenant Colonel Moses Parker*, an American officer.

No.3. *Samuel M'Clintock*, D. D., was born in Massachusetts, May 1, 1732; he graduated in 1751 at the college in New Jersey; Nov. 3, 1756, he settled as a minister in Greenland, New Hampshire, and died 27th April, 1804.

No. 4. *Major Willard Moore.*

No 5. *Major Thomas Knowlton*, of the Connecticut troops under Putnam; killed in 1776 in battle.

No. 6. *Major Andrew M'Clery*; killed by a cannon shot after the retreat.

No. 7. *Colonel William Prescott* was born at Groton, Massachusetts, in 1726; he was a lieutenant in the provincial forces at the capture of Cape Breton in 1758, and greatly distinguished himself on that occasion. He had the chief command at the battle of Bunker's Hill, and was among the last to leave the entrenchments. He resigned his commission in 1777, but was present as a volunteer at the capture of Burgoyne by Gates, in that year. He died Oct. 13, 1795.

No. 8. *General Joseph Warren* was born in Roxbury, Massachusetts, June 11, 1741; he received a liberal education, and in a few years became an eminent physician in Boston. He was very active in organizing resistance to British oppression, and a prominent member of the secret committee raised for that purpose. A few days before the battle of Bunker's Hill he was appointed a major-general, but served as a volunteer and was killed in the battle.

No. 9. *General Sir William Howe*, who succeeded Gage in the command of the British forces in America, arrived at Boston in May, 1775. He commanded at the Battle of Bunker's Hill. In September, 1776, he captured New York. On the 27th September, 1777, he took possession of Philadelphia, and on the 4th of October defeated the Americans at Germantown. In May, 1778, he was succeeded by Clinton. He died in 1814.

No. 10. *General Sir Henry Clinton*. He succeeded General Howe as commander-in-chief of the British forces in America, and returned to England in 1782. In 1795 he was governor of Gibraltar, and died Dec. 23, 1795.

No. 11. *Major John Small*, a British officer, and a friend of General Putnam, who saved the Major's life in this battle.

No. 12. *Colonel James Abercrombie*, a British officer; he was killed in the battle.

No. 13. *Major John Pitcairn* was the British officer who shed the first blood at Lexington. He was killed at the battle of Bunker's Hill by a negro soldier, as he mounted the parapet during the third attack. Major of marines.

No. 14. *Lieutenant Pitcairn*, an English officer, (son to the above.)

No. 15. *Lieutenant Francis Lord Rawdon*, born December, 1754, was made adjutant-general of the British army in America, 1778; in 1780 commanded one wing of Cornwallis's army at the battle of Camden; in 1793 was advanced to the rank of major-general; in 1812 was appointed governor-general of British India, and died 28th November, 1825.

No. 16. *Colonel Thomas Gardner*, a native of Brookline, Mass. He was mortally wounded while leading his men to reinforce the Americans.

No. 17. *Lieutenant Grosvenor*, accompanied by his faithful servant, who seems to look defiance to the whole British army, and is prepared and determined to be the messenger of death to any one who may attempt to hurt his young master, who is already wounded in the sword arm and breast.

General (then Colonel) *Stark*, though not designated in the plate, was in the battle; and at the head of his regiment from New Hampshire, twice compelled the enemy to retreat with dreadful loss. General Stark afterwards distinguished himself at the battles of Trenton and Bennington, and at the surrender of Burgoyne. He was a native of Londonderry, New Hampshire. He died May 8, 1822, in the 94th year of his age.

Captain (afterwards General) *Henry Knox*, at that time a bookseller in Boston, and commander of a company of grenadiers, was also in the battle as a volunteer. He died in Thomaston, Maine, Oct. 25, 1806, at the age of 56.

www.ingramcontent.com/pod-product-compliance
Lightning Source LLC
Chambersburg PA
CBHW020432010526
44118CB00010B/545